Reflection and Refraction

F. Khorsandjamal

For those rocks that rise to meet me,
thank you for the strength of your love and support.

With special thanks to Anj Smith, Caroline Charles and Graeme Cooke

Cover image – H. Khorsandjamal

Contents

Contents

Contents

Acceptance & Hope

Seven

Just seven steps,
A small number to climb

But these are the most challenging and rewarding
steps we can and will take if we choose to move forward

To keep going

Steps sadly worn away they are so well trodden,
Steep stone platforms that have become smooth and
slippery with age, treacherous for even the most well
accomplished navigator

A familiar journey that never seems to ease,
A different ache each time,
A path borne of pain

I seek encouragement in the knowledge of where they
lead to,
In the hands at my back as they urge and support me
to carry on

To not fall back

To continue toward a place of peace

Shock & Disbelief

The Call

"He's gone"

Irreversible

I can't hear,
I don't want to

I can't catch my breath,
I don't have a choice

I can't stand,
I don't need to

I can't cry anymore,
I don't stop

I can't forget,
I don't remember

Numb

You stifled my tears for so long, I didn't want or
know how to cry for you when the time came

Time and Space

I lay and looked up at a rectangle of sunlit,
cerulean, sky

A frame for your beauty

I watched as you flew in three perfect circles
and left the picture

I still wonder where you went

Inevitable

She reappeared in her dreams
She didn't know why

She spoke in silent words
She began to burn with despair

She finally took him away
She sank into an abyss

She said he would rise again with her
She begged him to wake up

She never came again
She had lost that love to her

Each Time

Each time we pass on the news, we go
through it again

Each time a different interpretation of
the pain and anguish

Each time an excruciating incision, a
permanent mark left behind

Denial

Searching

I continue howling into the moonlit blackness but still,
nothing comes back

The sound swallowed whole by the night

Resurrection

The ritual is over and the morning moon lies heavy
looking at me, the sun warm at my back

Yet again I had tried to piece you back together,
Bone by bone,
Dusk till dawn

Beating wings and breeze my prayer and meditation

A light that split the sky

The resuscitated realisation

Ebb

She would sit and search the silent skies
for a fairy tale, an alternate reality

Through haloed, windswept, clouds he would
come to her with the evening sun and kiss
her burning, tear stained, cheeks

A slow, fading, light

Amends

Was it you who surreptitiously entered my dreams,
The bird who night after night tried speaking to me in
confused, tender, song?

Mother

She burns
Her bones ache with grief

For now, all she craves is oblivion

Retrograde

I look at you through the lashing rains, the light
bright and blinding,
A strange stillness accompanying their sound,
A tranquillity

I travel with them, recall and reflect upon your
essence, your energy,
And when it comes to a stop you still linger

Here
Trapped

In glinting glass-like droplets caught on window
ledges and webs

Where I see the world inverted,
Where you still live

Blind

I would lie to myself so as not to lose you

Anger

For Whom

I heard three bells

And I screamed
And I screamed
And I screamed

Sometimes

Sometimes I resent you

Sometimes I think that you never wanted to stay

Sometimes I think that you didn't want to fight for
what you believed in

Sometimes I think you couldn't

Sometimes I think you took the easy way out

Sometimes

Hurt

You quietened me and left

A cruel, cowardly, and selfish departure

I have so much still to say
To resolve
To heal

Such gargantuan waves of anger flood my body
I fear I may drown in this silent rage before the
storm subsides

Pushed

He was too brilliant for you

That is the only explanation I can think of
as to why you could only look at him as splintered
sunlight through a loosely closed fist

Black

Today I woke wanting even birdsong banished

I want to scream into the still chambers of your heart

Unspoken

You were a fool who never understood me or tried to,
Who wronged me many times as a result but I still
loved you

I just wish you had allowed me the time to tell you

Holding

I am a pregnant thundercloud, fit to burst

Beast

Days, months, seasons, years, I spent wondering why
I should grieve, and did grieve eventually, someone I
despised so much,
Someone that had inflicted so much torment and torture
on those held closest

Days, months, seasons, years, came and went before I
could see what gifts you had given me, even in your taking,
And realised it was because you were simply a wounded
animal in great affliction, that only ever wanted and
needed to be loved

Dirt

You somehow entombed me in a fear so gripping
I travelled with it to the darkest parts of my being
and sank deep into quiet, black, earth

Solar Powered

I feel as though I stand at the centre of a solar system,
Implosion threatening,
Decimating all that exists within it or that dares enter

Sensitive

Did I need to be cruel and indifferent for you
to stay?

The Truth

When I look back, you never held dear the
things that I did

No recollection
No care

It hurts

Bargaining

Stay

I would have you haunt me forever, if it meant
having just something

Legacy

When I told the story of that 1500-year-old, life-giving
flame, I'd wished and willed my answer to the innocent
question that followed to simply

be

"Yes"

"Can it bring him back to life?"

Lightness

I wish I could have carried all that weighed
heavy in your heart,
I wish I could have left you holding light instead
and helped set you free

Guilt

Guilt

I still ask "Could I have done more?"

Intention

I thought my heart beat strong enough that
the reverberations would carry across aeons of
suffering to lift your own, damaged, heart

Not in this lifetime

Depression

Lost

Who am I grieving for, you or me?

Slave

What is this menace that won't allow me to heal,
To move forward,
To be free

That sits in the gloomy shadows of my soul,
That creeps through the crevices of my sub-conscious,
That seeps into streaming conscious thought,
That makes me feel I am so
Completely
And utterly
Unworthy

A bully that lies in wait,
A tormentor that strikes as soon as I choose to disobey
it and drags me back to where it has decided I belong

In the familiar comfort of pain

Preservation

I feel stuck, caught in the residue of death,
Slowly being enveloped by the heavy thickness,
Unable to muster the energy to resist

Resistance

Oh to let go of this longing for those now
lost to me, and to be liberated

Falling

The birds did not sing today

I listened to people, like susurrating autumn
leaves, speaking in hushed tones instead

Carnival of Black

My tears creak at first to escape then dance fiercely
and freely as they fall

Every vision and memory corrupted, made crooked, contorted

Until there is nothing left

The Visitor

Now you stand silently by her side,
But only in her dreams

Race to The End

It beats so hard and fast it beats me into a state of
paralysis,
Beating to breakthrough and escape my body but
tears are the only thing that leave me

Is this how you felt just before?

The Glass Box

I had seen it in my dreams long before,
Not knowing what it meant

On a perfect lawn, on a perfect day,
Dark, lush, trees either side,
Bright, inviting, sky above

The day
streaming
through

No entrance
No exit
A warm and silent solitary structure

Just one chair,
A lone seated figure

Black suit, head heavy bowed down

Waiting
Resigned

No other way out

Angustation

This perpetual fog that hangs, that shrouds me, is
suffocating, claustrophobic,
A thick, heavy, veil of misery I can barely see beyond

When will it lift?

Damaged

How do you mourn the living?

Cavern

I finally filled the vast, dark, empty, chamber that
lay within, flooding it with tears,
All the tears I never did or could cry,
So many I could no longer remember what they
were for or where they came from,
An endless streaming of sorrow

Harlequin

If only that masked mischief maker would
soundlessly dance out of my dreams and into reality,
To only have to tap and change the nightmare that
consumes me when I wake

The Future

She asked if things could ever be normal again

I said they would just be

Tower of Silence

Let me lay by your side and be carried to the skies

Emerald

Each day as twilight beckons,
When I see the familiar sight of those seven
parakeets passing by above,
A body of one,
Silhouetted against crepuscular light,
Each carrying a fragment of my grief,
Certain of their direction,
I yearn to fly with them

To Proceed

I wish I could just hit that button

'Accept and continue'

The Room

I enter into sunlit, warm, anguish,
Shrouded in silence

The clock is ticking,
Somewhere, tears begin to fall behind the closed door

I move to sit, slow and heavy

It's not you anymore

Human Matter

Nothing
Else
Matters
(Without you)

To Fall Asleep

I am utterly submerged
Gently
Drifting
Downwards

I gaze at the ethereal light from above that gradually
gives way to enveloping darkness

Hypnotised

Body weightless
Body heavy

How far will I have to fall?

The Void

I grieve the empty spaces left behind,
The empty spaces left on shelves and in between walls

I grieve the emptiness left inside me,
That emptiness which surrounds me,
The conversations left unspoken,
The laughter that will not be shared

I grieve the touch I will not feel

I grieve what was never there

Undone

Why must such precious, beautiful, things
have to destroy themselves

The Shell

A gust of wind that shook the beech tree,
The cawing crow, off course

Empty shoes on the ground

I realised you weren't here anymore

Dandelion Seed

You sailed away from us

A dandelion seed in the sun, floating out
of reach and out of sight,

Early nectar for the heavens

Come back

Acceptance & Hope

Acquiesce

I turn out the lights

I let the storm play out

Acknowledgement

There are demons borne of loss that can haunt
and terrorise us forever if we choose to let them

Or

We can look them in those torturous eyes
and try to befriend and understand them

Talk with them
Walk with them
Sit with them
Accept them

Let them go

Fantasy

Now that you are gone
I realise
You were never real to begin with

Amelioration

Raindrops on a rose trickle down my chin as I
draw it in to inhale the sweet, familiar, fragrance

My elixir

Antelucan

From time to time I feel this inexplicable and
overwhelming sadness,
Lifetimes of grief not realised that slowly creeps
then quickly crawls and clambers all over me,
permeating my soul,
A darkness that fills every fibre of my being with a
lament I feel I might never be able to let go of

But I sit patiently with it, I wait, I know it won't last
This enveloping obtenebration that embraces me in
it's wicked and wonderful arms,
This master of sorrows that teaches me something
new each time and stays with me till the dawn light,
Till I awaken

Eternal

I know you're there,
Somewhere,
Just like the sun,
Still shining behind the clouds

Endings

Now I see

And I learn to accept the many cruel and unexpected
forms in which death can visit us

Soothed

In the burning heat of night you came,
The cool, calming, breeze at my back

A comforting guide
A caring whisper

A quiet call to carry on

Polypodiopsida

The seasons changed and gradually you grew again
and uncoiled,
Unfurled your gentle fronds and stretched yourself fully,
Tips touching the spring sun,
Roots remediating the long-contaminated earth around
you

The Goldfinch

I quietly welcomed your greeting every day,
Sweet, lyrical, songs of everlasting hope

To Transcend

To me, it is only the heavenly heady scent of the
most beautiful flower that intensifies when the
rains have fallen

Confined

It took me a lifetime to realise I had enslaved
myself in order to protect you,
To be there for you in that closed room you held in
your heart and your head

That obligated child inside never growing up,
Never realising that I could choose to release and
protect myself at any time

The door too big and heavy to let myself out,
The only way, for my spirit to seek help in your
dreams and visions to push it open

I was never your saviour, your healer
I never could be

We were all orphaned, the children inside left to
stagnate and fend for ourselves,
Fragile psyches, broken hearts, pieces scattered
everywhere

But with freedom comes the hurt in learning to
let go of the relationship,
Of everything I know, an indescribable mutual loss

Time will heal, but for now we are trying to relearn
a new way of being,
And I must take pleasure in this pain as we make
the journey to progress

Peace

Sometimes we must let go of beautiful things,
To let them float away freely from us

Like a tiny, scarlet, maple leaf in the autumn
fallen on clear, dark, water,
Drifting divinely downstream

Gliding

The clouds pass quickly today, hazes of hurt dissipating

Retribution

I forgive you

Thistledown

You landed in my open palm

A gift
That was gently lifted by the air to rise again

A foot
above
my
head

And there you stayed for what seemed like
forever

A blessing
That gently lifted me to rise again

Sinistrorse

As the light increasingly grows, I finally realise I
haven't been going round in circles, but slowly
spiralling upward toward the sun

Inseparable

I feel that heaviness in my bones again,
That unease in the pit of my stomach,
Listless and heavy lidded

And I am thankful,
I am hopeful

Ready to appreciate the full depth of inevitable
lightness wedded to these gifts

Solace

I sat still, held by the long shadows of your
interlacing branches

Loved and supported

Gold dripping in between, crowning me
with peace

Birdsong to console

Unending

Even when he slowly span away from me,
we were always connected
He could see swifts in my words, flying in that
eternal circle

Dulciloquence

She could only hear his familiar, honeyed, mellifluous voice,
Somewhere, in the distance

"He's just gone ahead" came another

And she smiled in sad but sweet surrender

Multiverse

In letting go, I found softness
In softness, I found strength
In strength, I found space

And I could breathe again

I breathed deeply, inhaled all I could,
Inhaled a tiny universe of infinite, iridescent, light,
Inhaled a universe that had lay unrealised inside
of you

And I was happy that I could breathe life into it again

Faith

The sun's generously outstretched rays lightly hold me,
the warmth caressing my cheek and kissing me good
morning

I know it will be ok

Supported

You are not alone on this unsteady walk of grief,
From the most unexpected places, rocks will rise
to meet you

A Gift

I was given a heart, full of hope

Of treasures untold

Of secrets so precious

Of unbridled joy

Of rare acceptance and understanding

And I am encouraged to remind myself to look
inside at what has been lovingly bestowed,
To rediscover these gleaming, exquisite, things often

Trust

Just when I felt like I wouldn't stop falling,
I began to fly

Primrose

I spoke and you appeared,
Laughing,
Full of love and youth,
In a tilted half, yellow, moon

Acceptance

I was quietly disarmed

My fury and discontent quelled

The dark clouds passing peacefully by
beneath, giving way to higher visions of
electric orange and pink tinged passions

Hope

I look forward

To a place, a space in time, another dimension

Where we might talk,
Where we might hear,
Where we might see

And right all the wrongs we ever did to one another,
Commit them to a vault on the other side of the
universe, the other side of anything we know

I look forward

Dwelling

Maybe now, in the bare chambers of my heart, do
I feel ready to furnish them once again with whatever
new life, love and delight there is to surely come

You are loved.

Printed in Great Britain
by Amazon

40105120R00078